Koalas

The Real Story

Dr Mark Norman

OZ ANIMALS

black dog

First published in 2010 by

black dog books

15 Gertrude Street
Fitzroy Vic 3065
Australia
+ 61 3 9419 9406
+ 61 3 9419 1214 (fax)
www.bdb.com.au
dog@bdb.com.au

Designed by Ektavo Pty Ltd
Printed and bound in China by Everbest Printing International

National Library of Australia Cataloguing-in-Publication data:
Norman, Mark Douglas
Koalas: the real story / Mark Norman

Includes Index
For primary school age
Subjects: Koalas—Juvenile literature
ISBN: 9781742031309
Dewey Number: 599.25

10 9 8 7 6 5 4 3 2 1   10 11 12 13

AAP Images: pp 12, 13, 22, 24, 28, 39,
Shutterstock: front cover, pp i, ii, iii, 2, 3,
4, 5, 6, 7, 8, 9, 10, 11, 12, 14, 17, 18, 30;
Photodisk: p 4; Istockphoto: pp 15, back cover; BigStock Images:
pp 16, 25, 27; Photolibrary: pp 19, 23, 26; Auscape / Hedgehog
House: p 21; Chris and Sandra Pollitt/Antphoto: p 20

black dog books would like to thank Dr Kathrine Handasyde for
her thorough factual check of this book.

FSC is a non-profit international organisation
established to promote the responsible
management of the world's forests.

Contents

Up in the treetops

At the top of Australia's gum trees lives one of the country's strangest residents. It looks like a small bear but it's not a bear at all — it's the koala.

Koalas have lived in Australia for millions of years and have become experts at eating the **toxic** leaves of gum trees. Lots of things about koalas are strange. They have a pouch like a kangaroo, two thumbs per hand and a super-nose that can sniff out the toxins in leaves.

The **ancestors** of koalas were similar to wombats, but they grew to the size of small cars! The large ground **predators** of that time may have forced these **prehistoric** koalas to head for the safety of the treetops.

If you were a koala...
you would only eat gum leaves. If a human ate the same amount of gum leaves, they would be in a coma in ten minutes and dead within hours.

Where koalas live

Koalas live in southern and eastern Australia. They became **extinct** in Western Australia about 30 000 years ago.

Koalas live in gum trees. There are about 800 different types of gum tree, and koalas have favourite types of leaves that they like to eat. In northern Australia these are the Grey Gum and Tallowwood. In the south it is the Manna, Blue and Swamp Gums. In drier areas, they like the River Redgums.

A few things about koalas

Big ears with excellent hearing.

Weak eyesight with vertical pupils.

Sharp, ridged teeth for chewing tough leaves.

A small brain for thinking about chewing gum leaves.

Two thumbs per hand.

Joined fingers on the hindfoot used to comb the fur.

Mottled coloured rump for camouflage.

Round body for keeping in the heat.

Thick fur on the back for insulation, thin fur on the belly to let out the heat.

A button nose for smelling chemicals in gum leaves.

5

Strange food

Koalas are among the few animals in the world that can survive on gum leaves. Over millions of years they have developed a way to digest these leaves.

First they chew the leaves until they're like a gum-leaf smoothie. Koalas make acid in their liver to change the toxins in the leaves into harmless chemicals that are disposed of in their poo and wee.

Special **bacteria** live in a part of the koalas gut known as the **caecum** (see-kum). This bacteria also helps break down toxins. The caecum is like a very long, coiled-up tube — stretched out it would be six times longer than the koala!

Koalas normally don't drink water, because they get all the water they need from the leaves they eat. But when it gets very hot, or if there is a bushfire, they will climb down from the trees to look for water.

Super-sniffers

Different types of gum trees, and even leaves on the same tree, can have different amounts and types of poisons. This is where the koala's super nose comes in handy.

Koalas sniff the leaves and can tell without tasting which ones have too much poison. This way they can choose the best leaves or best trees.

Gum trees are also called **Eucalyptus** trees (you-ca-lip-tus). Their leaves are packed full of poisons called phenols (fen-ols) and terpenes (terp-eens).

If you were a koala...
you would eat about half a kilogram of gum leaves every day — about the same as one big box of breakfast cereal.

A day in the life of a koala

Because it takes so long to break down gum leaves in a koala's gut, most of a koala's life is spent sleeping.

Koalas are **nocturnal**, meaning they are more active at night. They begin feeding around dusk.

A normal day for a koala is:

6.00 p.m.	– Wake up, stretch, comb fur
7.00 p.m.	– Move to a new branch
7.04 p.m.	– Sniff leaves, start eating
9.00 p.m.	– Have a little rest
10.00 p.m.	– Comb your fur
11.00 p.m.	– Go to sleep
3.00 a.m.	– Wake, stretch, eat
5.00 a.m.	– Comb fur
6.00 a.m.	– Stretch, eat
7.00 a.m.	– Go back to sleep
12 noon	– Stretch, go back to sleep
3.00 p.m.	– Yawn, snore

If you were a koala...
you would spend on average
only four minutes a day travelling
somewhere!

Awkward acrobats

Koalas are great climbers. They can easily run up a tree trunk or telephone pole.

Koalas have to walk along the ground when they change trees. They don't like being out of the treetops because predators like **dingoes** can attack them when they're on the ground.

If you were a koala...
you would be able to walk straight up telephone poles.

Koalas climb by using their strong, sharp claws. They have two thumbs per hand, which gives them an excellent grip. They can make short leaps from branch to branch, but they have to be careful. It's a long way down if the branch snaps!

Surviving the weather

Special fur helps koalas survive in all kinds of weather.

The fur on the koala's back is thick and waterproof. In a storm they simply roll up in a tree fork and stay warm and dry.

Koalas can't sweat. When the weather gets hot, they stretch out and expose their thin belly fur, which lets the heat out. They also lick the fur over their wrists to cool down. When it gets super-hot they might even climb down to find a shady spot among the tree roots.

If you were a koala...
you would spend most of your life sitting naked on a tree branch, whether it was sunny, raining or snowing.

Koala talk

Koalas may look quiet, but they can actually make a lot of noise!

During breeding season, big males defend their **territories** by climbing to the treetops and bellowing at the top of their lungs. Females have high-pitched voices and will wail and scream if they don't want males near them.

Koala cubs make repeated high-pitch squeaks when they are distressed, especially when they lose track of their mothers.

If you were a girl koala...
you would snarl and scream. If you were a boy koala, you would roar and puff.

Fighting males

Male koalas like to live with lots of females, but will chase away other males.

A big male marks his trees with a special gland on his chest. He hugs a tree and rubs his chest on it. This leaves a greasy smear on the tree that gives off a sickly-sweet smell. Any new male coming along knows this area is already taken.

Sometimes males will fight. They wrestle by wrapping an arm around the shoulder of their opponent while trying to bite their elbows, ears and head. Sometimes koalas get deep wounds. They can even pull each other out of the trees!

If you were a male koala...
you'd rub smelly snot on all the corners of the house and around the garden to show people where you live.

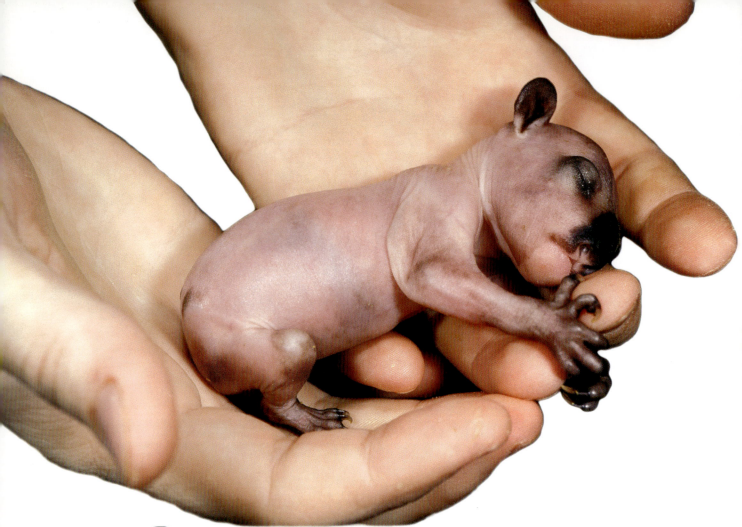

Amazing birth

Koalas have an incredible way of giving birth and raising their young.

The mother koala gives birth to a tiny naked baby, which is not much bigger than a human fingernail. The baby has no fur and its body is all arms and shoulders — it looks like a swimmer except its back legs aren't fully formed and it is almost blind.

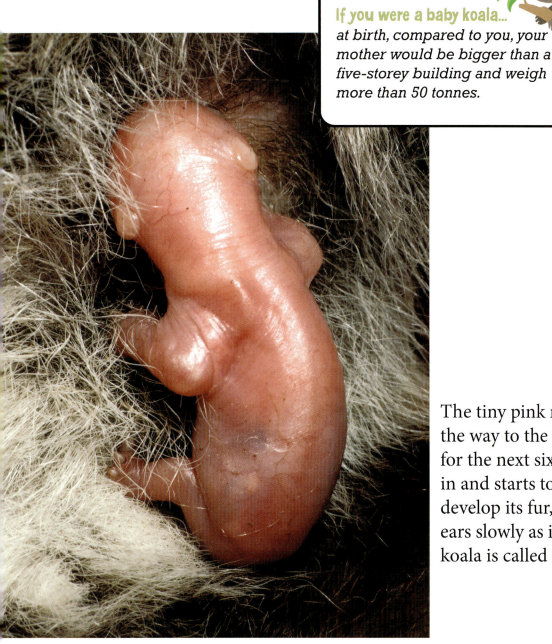

If you were a baby koala... *at birth, compared to you, your mother would be bigger than a five-storey building and weigh more than 50 tonnes.*

The tiny pink newborn crawls all the way to the pouch, its home for the next six months. It climbs in and starts to drink milk. It will develop its fur, back legs, eyes and ears slowly as it grows. A baby koala is called a joey.

Bringing up baby

About five months after being born, the baby koala finally opens its eyes and starts to stick its head out of the pouch.

The pouch is a safe place to live because it is warm and has all the milk a baby can drink. It's also safe from diseases because the mother produces an **antibiotic** slime in the pouch that prevents infections.

One of the strangest things about koalas is that the mother has to give her baby a special bacteria that will make its gut work when it begins to eat gum leaves. The baby does this by eating special poo from the mother called pap. Pap helps fill the baby's gut with the good bacteria. The baby has to eat pap for about an hour every two or three days.

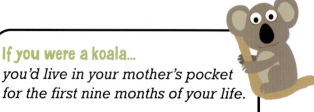

Out of the pouch

At about seven months of age, the young koala emerges to hang on to its mother's belly, before gradually moving onto her back.

Mother koalas sleep curled up with their babies hidden in their arms. The young now start tasting gum leaves given to them by their mothers. At nine months old, the young no longer return to the pouch.

By the time they are eleven months old, babies start to make short, wobbly trips away from their mothers. A female will sometimes slap an older baby if it tries to drink milk when a new baby is in the pouch.

Leaving home

At one year old, young koalas can finally fend for themselves.

As they get older, young male koalas are kicked out of their neighbourhood by adult males. The fights can be dangerous, and young males that refuse to go may fall and injure themselves.

Koalas are safest in the treetops. But treetops can also be a dangerous place for young koalas. They can fall out or be taken by powerful owls.

Koala conservation

Logging or clearing of land for farms and houses has taken away many of the places where koalas live.

Some koalas left in isolated forests have run out of gum trees to eat. In other places, koalas reproduce fast, leading to very high numbers. In the 1920s, 18 koalas were released onto Kangaroo Island in South Australia. In 1997 there were up to 27 000 koalas living there!

If there is too few koalas, they can't find each other to breed. If there's too many in a small area they eat too many leaves and cause the gum trees to die. Isolated populations can also have lots of problems with diseases.

One solution to these problems is planting **native** forests and making **wildlife corridors** to join different groups of koalas.

Koalas and climate change

As the climate changes, many areas in Australia are predicted to get hotter and the weather to get more extreme.

Hot weather leads to more bushfires that can threaten forests and the koalas that live in them. We all need to do as much as we can to fight climate change. We need to reduce our energy use and the way we treat the planet. Walk, recycle, reuse, plant trees and shop less. Find out more about what you can do to help.

If you were a koala...
you'd ask humans to plant more native trees, drive slowly and care for wildlife and the planet.

Glossary

antibiotic: a chemical substance that can destroy bacteria and other micro-organisms.

bacteria: types of single-celled creatures that can be either good or bad for other living creatures.

caecum: the part at the beginning of the large intestine.

dingo: a wild dog native to Australia.

Eucalyptus: a family of tall trees, mostly native to Australia. Their leaves contain oils that are poisonous and highly flammable.

extinct: no longer in existence, something that has died out.

native: born or belonging to a particular place or country.

nocturnal: an animal which is active during the night.

predator: an animal that hunts and eats other animals.

prehistoric: the time before recorded history.

territory: an area which an animal will defend against intruders, especially of the same species.

toxin: a poisonous substance.

wildlife corridor: also known as a green corridor. An area of habitat connecting wildlife populations that have been separated by human activity (such as farms, roads or logging).

Index

30